Starting the Entrepreneurial Journey

Verson 1.1

David Y. Choi. Ph.D.

Dedication

This book is dedicated to my mother, my entrepreneurial hero. Without any prior experience, she had the courage to start a small business to help support the family, including paying for my college education. She taught me valuable lessons about courage, hard work, sacrifice, family, and entrepreneurship that I now share with my students.

Dedication

Meet the Author

Professor David Y. Choi, Ph.D., is an educator, entrepreneur, advisor, and investor. Since 2003, he has taught entrepreneurship at Loyola Marymount University (LMU), where he holds the Conrad N. Hilton Chair of Entrepreneurship. Professor Choi is a recipient of the President's Fritz B. Burns Teaching Award, the highest teaching accolade at LMU. He is the author of *Growing Your Beautiful Small Business and a co-author of Values-Centered Entrepreneurs & Their Companies* and has published over 30 peer-reviewed academic articles. Born in South Korea, Professor Choi spent many years in Germany and Silicon Valley before settling in Los Angeles. He attended UC Berkeley and UCLA, obtaining degrees in engineering and business. His entrepreneurial journey includes founding and advising various startups in diverse industries such as food, consumer goods, software, and biotechnology, among others.

40.0%

"The percentage of times
I am wrong when students
ask me to judge their
business ideas."

– David Y. Choi, Ph.D.

Introduction

This book is designed for young (and young at heart) first-time entrepreneurs who want to kickstart their careers on the right foot.

I often wished that there was a book that I could give out to my new college freshmen entrepreneurship majors or even high school students visiting my university that could put them in the right mindset and path for an entrepreneurial career and approach to life. My intention was not to teach all of them how to start a business immediately. However, I thought that it was important for aspiring entrepreneurs to develop the right mindset and perspective as they initiate their entrepreneurial journey.

After all, entrepreneurship is about more than a startup! It's about having the right attitude toward life, self-belief, initiative, courage, determination, resilience, and discipline, which are the qualities that have enabled humans to accomplish great things throughout history.

To some extent, a startup is a byproduct of entrepreneurial individuals identifying and solving problems that lead to financial or social opportunities. In fact, there are great entrepreneurs in corporations, governments, and community organizations whose work does not result in a startup.

Of course, there is nothing wrong with startups. I find them to be a beautiful expression of one's mission, belief, competence, dedication, and character. I am confident that as long as people continue to dedicate themselves to building organizations for noble purposes, our world will be in great shape.

This book incorporates my thoughts and observations derived from over 20 years of researching and teaching entrepreneurship and advising entrepreneurs. It has been written to be easy to read and absorb, with our younger generation of readers—who are accustomed to TikTok and other attention-span-reducing social media—in mind.

I hope you find these lessons useful.

Many of these suggestions are supported by research, making them likely to be true. Some reflect my personal opinions aimed at stimulating your thinking, but none should be too far-fetched.

This book is not comprehensive, meaning there may be important lessons that are not covered within its pages. Many of the lessons focus on psychology, behavior, and work ethic, which constitute a significant portion, perhaps 80%, of what I believe is important for entrepreneurial success.

For further guidance on growing a small business, I encourage you to explore my book titled *Growing Your Beautiful Small Business. If you are interested in exploring how to build a socially responsible business*, please check out a book called Values-centered Entrepreneurs and Their Businesses, co-authored with my colleague Ed Gray.

David Y. Choi

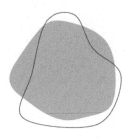

48 Lessons!

I can't possibly have more ideas.

Suggestion: Feel free to glance at all 48 lessons at once, but afterward, read one or two carefully each day to reflect and absorb.

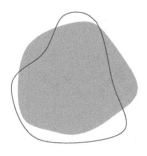

"May you always have a clean shirt, a clear conscience, and enough coins in your pocket to buy a pint!"

-Irish Proverb,
In honor of Professor Fred Kiesner, the first Conrad N. Hilton Chair of Entrepreneurship at Loyola Marymount University

"It is dangerous to make everyone go forward by the same road; worse to measure others by oneself."

- St. Ignatius of Loyola

He was quite smart for someone from the 16th century

"A life is not important except in the impact it has on other lives!"

-Jackie Robinson

and entrepreneurship is all about having a positive impact on people's lives

01

The Entrepreneurial Way of Life

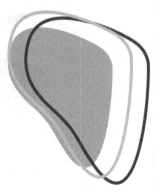

1.

Live, Don't Exist

"The proper function of a person is to live, not to exist ... I shall use my time."
– Jack London

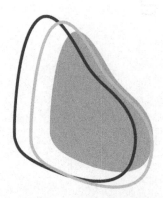

Welcome to entrepreneurship!

Entrepreneurship is not just a career path but a mindset and a way of life. It's a lens through which you view the world.

Problems become opportunities for change, profit, better relationships, and, most importantly, your chance to make a difference. You don't mind hardship. In fact, you know that crises offer special opportunities for your heroic action.

Being an entrepreneur also means living proactively. It's about crafting a life with minimal regrets. You take initiative, and your thoughts turn into actions. No one needs to tell you what to do.

You don't just follow the crowd; you think for yourself. You don't let irrational rules or traditions hold you back. You're primed to break boundaries and innovate.

Giving up isn't in your vocabulary; you embody grit and resilience. You find innovative ways to overcome challenges. When things don't work out, you try something different. Each failure is nothing but a learning opportunity.

Interested in pursuing your dream of a great, rewarding life with lots of achievements? Don't waste another minute. Steve Jobs once said in a college graduation speech: "Your time is limited, so don't waste it living someone else's."

Let's aim to live a fruitful life while making a positive impact on the world. You may be young, but there is never enough time. Most older people would pay millions to be younger if they could. In other words, your time is worth millions of dollars, so let's not waste it.

Takeaway: Strive to live a life of meaning and impact, starting today!

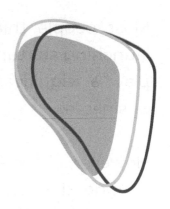

2.
Entrepreneurship is about More Than a Startup

"All humans are entrepreneurs not because they should start companies but because the will to create is encoded in human DNA."
– Reid Hoffman

Most people think entrepreneurship is just about launching startups. Of course, entrepreneurship does play a significant role in starting and building businesses.

However, I have also seen corporate managers make a huge difference by changing the direction and culture of their companies and exhibiting incredible entrepreneurial leadership in the process. Similarly, I have observed young women and men demonstrating strong entrepreneurial capabilities as they work to turn around the struggling family businesses that their parents or grandparents started.

Actually, I see great entrepreneurship everywhere. I've observed entrepreneurs among teachers, government officials, volunteers, and community organizers. I've also noticed that some of my neighbors mobilizing others to join in their efforts to improve the environment are great entrepreneurs.

One of the most remarkable entrepreneurs in history is Mother Teresa, who started orphanages and leprosy homes, not startups. But she exhibited more entrepreneurial passion and talent than almost anyone else on the planet. She was a fabulous social entrepreneur.

It might sound surprising, but I observe entrepreneurial talent among some of my faculty colleagues who identify interesting problems to research, exhibit remarkable grit when experiments go wrong, and eventually invent innovative solutions.

Many scholars still debate who or what an "entrepreneur" truly is, but there is little doubt that anyone can benefit from being more entrepreneurial in their lives.* You can have a more rewarding life by having a purpose, taking action, and living your life to the fullest. When you feel ready, you can start an organization of some kind, whether it's a student club, a community group, or even a startup.

Takeaway: Enrich your life by being an entrepreneur (of some kind)!

*Gartner, W. B. (1988). "Who is an entrepreneur?" is the wrong question. American journal of small business, 12(4), 11-32.

3.
It's About the Mindset

If you want to kill a big dream, tell it to a small-minded person."
— Steve Harvey

This may surprise some readers. Successful entrepreneurs are not necessarily smarter or have higher IQs than others. Moreover, although accomplished entrepreneurs do have knowledge relevant to their businesses, that is generally not what distinguishes them from others, such as less stellar entrepreneurs or employees of large organizations.

What truly distinguishes successful entrepreneurs is how their minds work. When you observe them, you will find certain commonalities: They tend to be (sometimes unreasonably) optimistic and energetic, and they don't seem to get discouraged easily. They believe in themselves and fully trust that their hard work will pay off in the end. They often make mistakes, but their missteps or even failures don't seem to stop them. In other words, they have a different mindset.

In fact, studies have indicated that developing the right mindset can be more powerful for entrepreneurs than even having business knowledge. Professor Alex Glosenberg at LMU argues that having an entrepreneurial mindset means being proactive, innovative, and resilient all at the same time. Equally fascinating, we are learning that people can adopt this new mindset relatively quickly, often in just weeks.

Being proactive means taking initiative. It means that you often act before being told to do so by someone else (e.g., parents or your boss) and usually before others do. If you find yourself initiating actions among your friends or doing things before your parents get on your case, you might be quite proactive.

Being innovative means doing things differently. You might be someone who thinks outside the box or finds creative solutions to problems. If not, no worries. Innovativeness is a muscle that you can exercise and strengthen over time.

Being resilient means pursuing your goals even when you experience setbacks. Resilience does not mean being "tough." Some of the most resilient people are those who meditate, pray regularly, or have good emotional support from family and friends.

Anyone who is proactive, innovative, and resilient all at once is likely to be quite an entrepreneur. Moreover, you can improve on any or all of these areas and become an even more powerful entrepreneur over time!

Takeaway: Strengthen your entrepreneurial mindset: Strive to be more proactive, innovative, and resilient.

*Campos, F., Frese, M., Goldstein, M., Iacovone, L., Johnson, H. C., McKenzie, D., & Mensmann, M. (2017). Teaching personal initiative beats traditional training in boosting small businesses in West Africa. *Science*, 357(6357), 1287-1290.

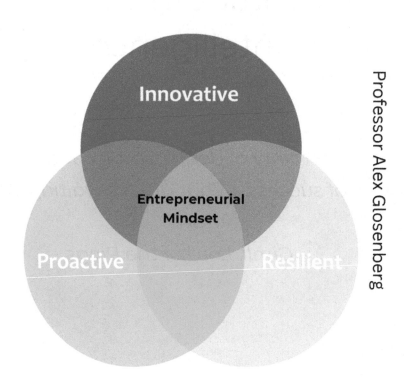

Professor Alex Glosenberg

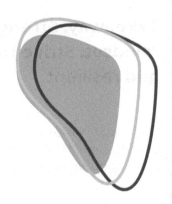

4.
Attitude Trumps Intelligence

"Certainty of death, small chance of success...What are we waiting for?"

— Gimli, Lord of the Rings

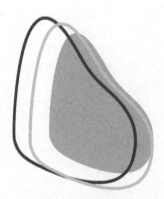

Based on my observations of my students' careers over the years, I've learned that attitude, a clear and direct reflection of one's mindset, is often the biggest difference-maker in the career trajectories of my former students. A young person with a great attitude toward personal growth and work, coupled with energetic vibes and an optimistic outlook, easily outshines someone with a higher IQ or academic record. I've found that someone with a good attitude eventually develops the competencies they need to rise to the top in their organization.

I once had an undergraduate student whom I invited to join a business competition team because he was a good presenter. However, on the day before we were leaving for a national competition, he decided to recreate the team's financial model and ended up making it far worse. I scolded him for wrecking the financial model that we had to present the next day. Most students would have resented my tone of voice.

I immediately felt bad for raising my voice, but the student's response made me feel even worse. He said, "Thank you so much for teaching me this. I want to learn and get better." It was then that I realized he was more mature in attitude than I was.

It's no surprise that this former student has had an incredible career as an executive at some of the hottest startups in the U.S. He has also become a recognized name in brand marketing, a field in which he worked passionately to develop his expertise.

He was not the brightest student, but it didn't matter. His colleagues told me that he was an inspirational leader. Years later, when I met with him, he had become so knowledgeable about his field that he seemed incredibly brilliant. Nothing is more powerful than a great attitude.

Takeaway: Let your positive attitude shine through in everything you do.

from Deviantart.com

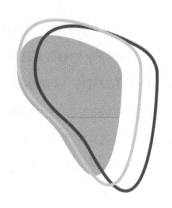

5.
You Can't Do Everything That You Put Your Mind To (or Can You?)

"I am not bound to win, but I am bound to be true. I am not bound to succeed, but I am bound to live by the light that I have."
– Abraham Lincoln

Can anyone build a successful company? Well, probably not, although I wish it were so. However, I am constantly surprised by how many people actually can! Not everyone can become a multi-billionaire like Elon Musk, but I find that most of my hard-working former students lead more than comfortable lives as business owners. I am often surprised at how frequently I underestimated people (students and others) around me in the past: Many individuals who I thought would have difficulty have become success stories.

Professor Peter Drucker, one of the brightest minds in the field of business, made it clear: "Most of what you hear about entrepreneurship is all wrong. It's not magic; it's not mysterious, and it has nothing to do with genes. It's a discipline, and like any discipline, it can be learned."

It can be learned!

I agree. To a large extent, it's like any discipline—like marketing, karate, or mathematics. Even if you can't be world-class, you can become quite good if you put in the effort. And being quite good is enough to find success and wealth in business ownership or other forms of entrepreneurial pursuit.

I remember a college friend of mine. A year or two into his startup, I visited him at his work and thought that there was no hope for him as an entrepreneur. He was quite bad at almost everything. But over the years, he's learned many of the skills needed for his business to thrive. Today, he pays for all the bills when our friends get together for dinner and drinks. It's another evidence that business is not rocket science, and you don't have to be a genius to make a good living at it.

Your parents were right after all. You can do almost anything that you set your mind to.

Takeaway: Devote yourself to the discipline of entrepreneurship to achieve your dreams.

6.
Find Your Purpose (at least take a good guess)

"The two most important days in your life are the day you were born and the day you found out why."
– Mark Twain

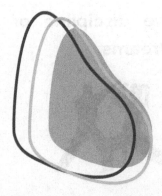

So, what is your purpose in life? What's your calling? How will you make a difference? Will your entrepreneurial pursuits fulfill that purpose? Do you need to start a business to pursue your purpose, or will you join an organization where you can make an impact? These are difficult questions, and your college (or early adult) years are a great time to contemplate them.

If you are an adult who didn't get to ponder these questions in college or your younger years, it's not too late to do it now and at least identify a general direction.

Brad Keywell (EY Entrepreneur of the Year for the U.S. and the World, and a former student of the legendary LMU Professor Fred Kiesner) often compares entrepreneurs to artists who have an irresistible need to create. If you have such a compelling passion for startups, you are one of the lucky ones. You would be pursuing a profession that is your calling and can make a difference in the world.

Also fortunate are those people who just *know* what they want to do with their lives. Some people seem to know from an early age that they want to be artists, doctors, or engineers and never change their minds. The rest of us, however, need time to discover our talents, beliefs, passions, and desires to find our purpose and suitable career options.

One of the best exercises you can do to find your future career is to examine your Ikigai—a concept that originated in Okinawa, Japan. Ikigai can be so powerful for setting one's direction that it has even been partially credited with contributing to the happiness and longevity of the Okinawan people.

Your Ikigai is the intersection of what you love to do, what the world needs (or more accurately, what you think the world needs), what you are good at, and what you can be paid for. See the next page for a diagram. Take the time to conduct this exercise and discover your Ikigai.

Of course, the challenge is that you often don't know what the world needs, what you are good at (if you haven't tried many things), or what the world will pay you for. You aren't even sure what you love. This is where life experiences come in. To develop such experiences, it's a good idea to try a number of of jobs and/or internships. It's common for young people to have interests in a wide range of interests, from movies, fashion, sports, finance, to technology, without knowing what the daily work entails, what people in these professionals are like, and what financial rewards await in these industries.

I hope that all readers find their Ikigai.

While searching for it, I hope that young people will awaken to the need and their capability to make the world a better place. Our world needs young people who care about the planet and its various inhabitants.

Takeaway: Find your purpose/Ikigai. The world depends on it.

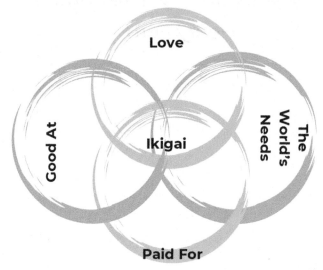

7.
Confidence is a Decision

"Whether you think you can or think you can't – you're right."
– Henry Ford

I once heard Russell Wilson, a Super Bowl-winning NFL quarterback, mention on a late-night TV show that his father used to ask him, "Why not you?" to challenge him to believe in himself. Many psychologists now believe that confidence—the capacity to trust in one's abilities and think positively—is a skill that can be developed and improved. This skill often involves ignoring your worst enemy and naysayer—usually your own inner voice.

I've had former students who achieved remarkable success, becoming CEOs of companies before the age of 30. Interestingly, I've also seen stellar former students, brilliant and hard-working, end up working as secretaries five years after graduation. The key difference seems to lie not in their intellect or competence, but in their levels of self-confidence and expectations of themselves.

Russell Wilson's father had it right. It's a great exercise to ask yourself, "Why not you (me)?" Wilson was considered undersized as a quarterback at both the collegiate and professional levels. Telling yourself "I can do this" and thinking positively and confidently can absolutely increase your chances of reaching your dream.

Legendary soccer player Cristiano Ronaldo agrees: "If you don't believe you are the best, then you will never achieve all that you are capable of."

If you keep asking yourself, "Why not me? Why couldn't I do XYZ?" you might reach a point where you ask yourself the inevitable question, "But do I know how to do XYZ?" At that point, your answer should not be "no," but "not yet."

The fact is, no billionaire entrepreneurs knew exactly what they were doing when they got started. Their answers to the question "Do you know what you are doing?" would have been "no" at many points in their careers, but they didn't let their lack of knowledge discourage them. They simply figured things out over time.

Don't limit yourself by answering with a "No"; instead, confidently say "Not yet," followed by "I will figure it out." You can fail in life despite having confidence, but without it, you have no chance.

Takeaway: Why not you? Believe in yourself first, and then work on the rest.

*Bandura, A., & Locke, E. A. (2003). Negative self-efficacy and goal effects revisited. *Journal of Applied Psychology*, 88(1), 87–99.

8.
Working Hard is a Talent

"Discipline is doing what you hate to do, but doing it as you love it"
– Mike Tyson

Every employee I ever let go for not working hard had one thing in common: They all thought they were working hard. Many people mistakenly or wishfully believe that they are working hard, even when most others wouldn't think so.

People often perceive intelligence as an innate talent, while hard work is seen as something anyone can do on a whim if they want to. So, can anyone who wants to work hard actually do so effectively? Sir Alex Ferguson, the legendary manager of the Manchester United football team, often explains that being able to work hard is a talent—a view increasingly more psychologists actually agree with.

Like any talent, you need to nurture it. The idea of working 10 or more hours a day might seem challenging at first for most young people. Most entrepreneurs I know are used to working 12 hours a day and do it very effectively. I know that this lifestyle is not healthy for the long term, but I used to think that if I woke up in the morning and wasn't tired from the previous night's hard work, I probably wouldn't give my best. The idea of working long hours can seem old-fashioned and unintelligent. However, for a young person, long hours can also mean accelerated learning.

I once worked as a consultant in two offices, one that required me to work 8 hours a day and the other that pushed me to work 16 hours a day. There is no doubt that I learned more and became a better professional in the office where I averaged 16 hours each day.

Many of my students launched their startups right after college, but some of the most successful entrepreneurs have been those who worked for 2-3 years before starting their companies. I believe those work experiences were quite helpful in training them to work with discipline.

Finally, hard work also means sacrificing leisure activities that most people value, such as hobbies, picnics, golf games, etc. I once heard Serena Williams, the legendary tennis player, say that she had "sacrificed friends" for her success because she couldn't have a normal teenage life. I can't think of anything more certain than sacrifice when it comes to progress. What are you willing to sacrifice?

Takeaway: Success comes from hard work and sacrifice – the two proven ingredients for success.

*Ulrich, D., & Smallwood, N. (2012). What is talent? Leader to Leader, 2012 (63), 55-61.

9.

You Are What You Spend Your Time On

"As a man sow, shall he reap."
– Bob Marley
(adapted from Galatians 6:7)

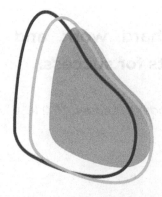

People often say you are what you eat, and it's probably true. We are all products of our environment and our actions. Over the last two decades, I've had a front-row seat to this observation: Some college freshmen, essentially beginners, develop into impressive, mature professionals by their senior year, while others remain immature and unemployable at the time of graduation.

The difference can largely be attributed to one simple factor: the amount of time spent on personal and professional growth. Students who paid attention in class, participated in professional development workshops, attended speaker events to meet entrepreneurs and leading professionals, secured internships, and worked on entrepreneurial projects during their college years were on their way to becoming success stories. On the other hand, those who spent too much time on fraternity/sorority activities or video games simply did not mature as professionals.

What you spend your time on and with whom you spend it really matters. Most people have heard of the 10,000-hour rule, which suggests that if you work diligently on a specific skill for 6-7 years (assuming you work about 1,500 productive hours a year), you can become exceptionally proficient at it.

How long does it take for a brilliant attorney at a law firm to become a partner? Usually 6-7 years. How long does it take for universities to determine that a new faculty member is ready for tenure? Again, 6-7 years. Interestingly my observation has always been that it takes about that long for a new owner of any business to become established.

Again, business is not rocket science. Most people who dedicate themselves become quite good at it.

There is a caveat: You need to develop your skills at the right time. It's much more valuable to hone your skills for launching a startup or becoming a first-year law firm associate at 25 than at 45. Our world tends to welcome a 25-year-old entrepreneur or law firm associate but not a 45-year-old one. So, don't believe it when people say, "You have time."

Takeaway: Dedicate (a lot of) your time to developing your entrepreneurial talents!

10.
Don't Dwell on Your Disadvantage(s)

"I have had all of the disadvantages
required for success."
– Larry Ellison

There is no shame in having grown up with a disadvantaged background. No reasonable person will look down on someone for having started poor or having faced other disadvantages not within their control.

That's not to say that disadvantaged backgrounds don't come with serious hindrances or that economic, racial, ethnic, or gender discrimination doesn't exist. They do. Thus, it's important to learn history and understand how certain people have been historically mistreated. It's also crucial to grasp how societal forces shape us as individuals, families, and communities.

I myself used to complain about discrimination. But one day I had to face this particular reality: Some people with similar and even worse childhoods than mine found a way to succeed. Some even used their early misfortunes as motivation and drive for their achievements.

It would be futile for a group of people to assume that they are predestined to fail. It can't be productive to presuppose that people will disrespect you because of your race or gender. In fact, studies of successful people often indicate that they have a strong internal locus of control, meaning they believe they are in charge of their destiny, whether it's entirely true or not.*

Successful entrepreneurs tend to be "opportunity-oriented," meaning they focus on possibilities rather than their limited resources. In fact, the very first widely-used academic definition of entrepreneurship was "the process by which individuals pursue opportunities without regard to the resources they currently control."**

As an entrepreneur, you've got to believe that you can influence your fate. At the end of your life, you need to be able to say: "I have fought the good fight, I have finished the race, I have kept the faith" (2 Timothy 4:7). These points are also reaffirmed by Nelson Mandela, who, after spending 26 years in jail, still believed, "I am the master of my fate and the captain of my destiny."

Takeaway: Be the master of your destiny.

*Lau, V. P., & Shaffer, M. A. (1999). Career success: The effects of personality. *Career Development International,* 4 (4), 225-231.

**Stevenson, H. H., & Jarillo, J. C. (2016). A new entrepreneurial paradigm. In *Socio-economics* (pp. 185-208). Routledge.

11.
Cultivate a
Reputation

*"It takes 20 years to build a
reputation and 5 minutes to ruin
it."*
– Warren Buffet

No matter what you do, whether you enter college or start a business, you must strive to cultivate a positive personal reputation. Perhaps you want to be known for your reliable work ethic, creativity, or integrity. Whatever your reputational goal, once you've established it among your peers, customers, or business partners, your work becomes significantly easier. Whether you are looking for a job or seeking funding for your startup, a stellar reputation will be a huge asset for you.

Take the case of Jensen Huang, co-founder and CEO of NVIDIA. His reputation as one of the company's best engineers convinced his boss, Wilfred Corrigan, founder of LSI Logic, to facilitate a meeting between Huang and Don Valentine, a prominent venture capitalist. Impressed by Huang's track record and driven demeanor, Valentine invested in NVIDIA. Huang has been known to say, "You can't run away from your past, so have a good past."

One thing you don't ever want to be known for, even among your closest friends, is being dishonest in any way. As a student, it's far better to flunk a test than to let your high school or college buddies see you cheat. Those friends, no matter how close, will not entrust you with important jobs or business opportunities in the future. Your business partners who've seen you do anything inappropriate will not vouch for you for future business opportunities.

You also don't want to be known as someone lazy, selfish, or unreliable by failing to fulfill your responsibilities. I've seen some of my students ruin their professional reputations by flaking on their college group projects. They might say to themselves, "It's not real work, just a class project," but you may get branded as someone unreliable. Since people's perceptions of others seldom change over time, you may find yourself wondering, 10 years later, why none of your friends are contacting you about great jobs or entrepreneurial opportunities.

The foundation for your reputation ("personal brand") starts with honesty and diligence. Of course, being known as a nice, friendly, mature, or loyal person also helps a great deal. Don't tarnish your reputation early in your career by being dishonest or lazy.

Takeaway: Cultivate a reputation for yourself as an honest and hardworking individual.

12.

Carve Your Own Path

*"I took the one less traveled by, and
that has made all the difference."*
– Robert Frost

Let's say that you know what you want to do with your life. Some young people actually do. Perhaps it's a career path that is not pursued by many of your friends, something less common or slightly riskier.

When your parents or friends suggest that you might be headed in the wrong direction and advise you to consider doing something else—such as getting a government job, a position in an investment bank, or attending law school—it's natural to question yourself and wonder if you're making the right decision. After all, it's lonely to be the only one among your friends doing something different. It can seem easier to have the same jobs as your friends and be miserable together.

However, you may find comfort in Bronnie Ware's book Have No Regrets: A Life Transformed by the Dearly Departing, that the No. 1 regret among dying adults is, "I wish I had pursued my dreams and aspirations, not the life others expected of me."

When I was young, I recall being affected by what people said. I remember being bothered, even losing sleep over it. Decades later, I honestly can't recall why other people's opinions used to matter so much.

It makes no sense. As I've grown older, my respect has shifted to those who carve their own career paths, regardless of their position or income.

Take, for example, my friend Tom, who never sought a traditional job despite parental and peer pressures. True to himself and his ambitions, he chose to work for himself, travel, and remain a bachelor. He may not have had a great stable income, but as an entrepreneur and traveler, he's lived one of the most interesting lives I know.

Certainly, we should all be open-minded and consider others' viewpoints, but don't let their definitions of success dictate your actions. Avoid letting friends, parents, or teachers sway you from following your heart.

Takeaway: Don't fear taking the road less traveled.

Ware, B. (2011). *Have no regrets: a life transformed by the dearly departing.*

02

Preparing for Your Startup

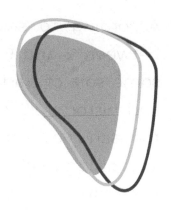

13.
Startup - No Time Better in Human History

"You don't have to be great to start, but you have to start to be great."
– Zig Ziglar

According to scientists, the earliest humans lived between 2 and 6 million years ago. There was likely some sort of trading ("business") a million years ago, and history tells us that there were great merchants thousands of years ago. But whether you examine the last million years or just the most recent 30 years, there has never been a better time to be a startup entrepreneur than now!

Consider the opportunities. How many more opportunities have been created in the last 30 years because of the Internet? How many new apps have been launched thanks to the smartphone? Approximately 10 million by 2023. How many new ideas and millionaires are emerging nowadays (2024) because of AI? The number of promising ideas and eventually successful companies is at an all-time high.

Then, think about the financing resources available. U.S. venture investments in 2021 hit a record high of $345 billion, offering funding to about 19,000 companies. Although the number of investments dropped significantly in the last two years, in 2023 15,766 deals were recorded, indicating that if you had a good startup, you could raise financing and have an income while pursuing your dream.

If you aren't ready for venture capital right away, there are alternatives. Today's abundance of incubators, accelerators, angel investors, business advisors, community development financial institutions, and entrepreneurship education programs is unprecedented. For those who have built thriving companies, business brokers, financial advisors, and private equity firms offer lucrative deals.

With each passing decade, the amount of new wealth generated from the sale of companies appears to increase exponentially. Whether you're the founder or an early employee, being with the right startup can provide a fulfilling career and substantial financial rewards.

What are the risks of venturing into startups these days? What risk? Entrepreneurs who don't succeed are often gobbled up by large companies that value employees with passion and a history of initiative. In some cases, your startup experience can be a resume builder for corporate jobs later. It's clear – this is the golden era for startups.

Takeaway: Consider starting or joining a promising startup!

14.

Believe in the Positive Power of Business

"Entrepreneurship is a shovel you use to dig a path to a brighter future."
– Jeff Hoffman

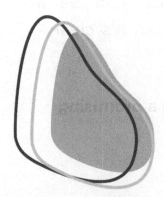

We often hear in the news about the malevolent side of business – there's no denying that some businesses are led by unscrupulous individuals. However, the lion's share of businesses, ranging from local family-owned shops to many prominent corporations, are helmed and operated by individuals with noble intentions. Most entrepreneurs and corporate leaders work tirelessly to serve their customers, employees, and communities, all while providing for their own families.

For many of today's entrepreneurs, their businesses represent not just a source of income but also a vehicle for self-expression and a tool (like a shovel) to carve a path to a brighter future. There are countless examples of responsible entrepreneurs who have excelled in developing superior products for their customers while taking excellent care of their employees, community, and even the environment. Take, for example, Newman's Own, a salad dressing company started by the legendary actor and race car driver Paul Newman. The company donates 100% of its profit to charity and is known for having given more than $500 million over the years. As you contemplate starting a company, I urge you to consider building one with a noble purpose – one that truly reflects your values and can serve as an example to others.

There is nothing wrong with money; in fact, it's great to have it. But if you build a great business, you can make money responsibly while making a positive impact on the world.

Life gets generally easier when you maintain a positive view of the world – when you believe that people are (or can be) essentially good, that capitalism works more than half of the time, that hard work will eventually pay off, and that businesses can play a positive role in our society. As Paul Orfalea, founder of Kinko's and a noted lecturer at LMU, aptly puts it: "You can't make money with a sinister view of the world."

Takeaway: Build your business to be a force for good.

*Choi, D & Gray, E. (2010). *Values-Centered Entrepreneurs and Their Companies.*

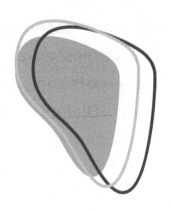

15.
Sharpen Your Empathy to Identify Opportunities

"You should not judge; you should understand."
– Ernest Hemingway

It's very common for entrepreneurs to start their companies as a result of addressing problems they have personally experienced. A notable example is Sara Blakely of Spanx, who redesigned her undergarments after finding the original design restrictive and uncomfortable. Her innovation became the foundation for her successful company.

However, note that the problems from which great ideas originate don't need to be your own. If you are empathetic and can relate to the pains and feelings of others, you will be able to identify many more problems and, in the process, discover a number of great entrepreneurial opportunities.

I wouldn't be surprised if scientists discover someday that empathy and sympathy are forms of intelligence superior to analytical reasoning—attributes traditionally gauged by instruments like IQ tests.

With the rise of artificial intelligence handling a vast majority of analytical tasks, one might wonder about the relevance of human analytical capabilities. In fact, it is quite uncertain what role humans will play and which job will persist.

.

The good news is that the world, even in the age of automation, will never run out of problems demanding solutions. Those who are empathetic and thereby adept at identifying important problems of their own and others and can craft appropriate solutions to those problems will never run out of work.

Moreover, those entrepreneurs who can utilize their empathy to encourage and motivate others to join their cause will be our future leaders. They will be the ones creating jobs and initiating the changes that we will see in the future.

In summary, the ability to understand and connect with others will be crucial.

Takeaway: Truly understanding and connecting with people can unveil untapped opportunities.

16.

Discover a Good Problem

"A problem well stated is a problem half-solved."
– Charles Kettering

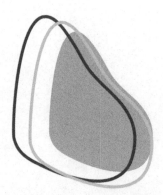

Every week, students approach me with their business ideas. As I listen, I often find myself asking, "Wait, what's the problem you're trying to solve again?" I ask this not to be provocative, but because the proposed idea sometimes lacks clarity—understandable, as 20-year-olds often don't have extensive business experience. However, sometimes the underlying problems that students identify are indeed intriguing and novel.

I recall Brandin Cohen, a co-founder and CEO of Liquid IV, telling me, at the time of founding the startup, that he thought there was a problem with the existing methods of hydration. He noticed that many young people in their 20s and 30s when they exercised or suffered from hangovers, consumed Pedialyte, an electrolyte drink designed and mostly used to rehydrate little children suffering from diarrhea. He and his co-founders went on to develop a solution to the identified problem that became a billion-dollar company.

To an observer, it might seem easy to clearly grasp and articulate a problem or an unmet need, but this task can be quite hard. To truly grasp the core issue, once you've identified a potential problem, you often need to delve deeper by repeatedly asking, "Why is this a problem?". This method of questioning is often referred to as root cause analysis — a well-established and effective technique.

Once the problem is clear in one's mind, there's a good chance of developing the right solution. Indeed, identifying the exact problem can be both the most demanding and exhilarating aspect of developing a new product or initiating a startup.

Finding a significant problem is so crucial that some investors actively search for substantial, yet unresolved issues around the world. Legendary entrepreneur and investor Vinod Khosla explains: "To me, any big problem is a big opportunity. If there is no problem, there is no solution, and there is no company. No one will pay you to solve a non-problem."

Takeaway: Find a good problem and get a good grasp of it.

17.

Formulate the Right Solution

"It is much easier to come up with technology that people don't want than to come up with ideas that people want."
– Steve Jobs

Once you've identified a good problem (at least in your estimation) and understood the underlying needs, it's time to start envisioning what your solution might look like. At this stage, you don't have to build the product or start coding. Instead, take a pencil and paper (or open up a drawing software) and sketch out your solution.

With some sketches in hand, it's generally a good time to discuss your idea with others. Contrary to conventional wisdom, speaking to as many people as possible about your idea can be highly beneficial.

While there are rare cases where someone might steal your idea, most people are not interested in appropriating someone else's concept to spend years developing it. In general, sharing your idea widely can lead to valuable feedback and improve your concept.

Incorporating feedback often involves letting go of certain aspects of your initial ideas and setting aside your pride. This iterative process can refine your idea and increase its potential for success. Continuing with the story of Liquid IV, the initial concept was a bottle filled with electrolyte liquid just like the competing products Pedialyte, Gatorade, and Powerade.

However, as the co-founders discussed the idea with others, it became evident that the initial concept might be less feasible than they had thought. Competing head-on with established brands using a similar format would have been a perilous strategy. Fortunately, a suggestion from another past student and accomplished marketer, Ruben Dua, led the co-founders to shift their focus to a powder form. This adjustment not only differentiated the startup from the competition but also significantly enhanced its profit margins.

While it took about nine years of effort to achieve success, the initial conversations and the resulting product design direction were pivotal in Liquid IV's path to becoming a billion-dollar enterprise.

Takeaway: Strive to develop the most effective solution by sharing your idea with others.

18.
Fear No Failure

"Doubt kills more dreams than failure ever will."
– Suzy Kassem

Let's face it: It's very likely that the biggest failure you will experience in life is regretting not doing something because you were too afraid, or worse because you had doubts about yourself. I've watched ultra-intelligent individuals remain paralyzed by self-doubt and fear of failure to the extent that they couldn't pursue their passions or start projects that could have changed their lives.

I certainly understand people who find themselves in situations where they cannot afford to have unreliable income for an extended period. For instance, some people I know need their consistent salaries to support their parents and siblings each month.

It's more difficult to comprehend why some people who are miserable with their jobs don't pursue something different. As Virginia Satir noted, perhaps they are people who "prefer the certainty of misery to the misery of uncertainty." In short, they are so fearful of the uncertainty and the risk of making a bad decision that they choose to remain in their miserable situation. Psychologists note that many people engage in something called "catastrophic thinking", i.e., the habit of ruminating about irrational, worst-case outcomes.

These folks worry that their entrepreneurial project could pan out so badly that they might lose their business, house, spouse, children, and end up on the streets.

When I ask these folks how many catastrophic entrepreneurial stories they have personally witnessed among their friends, the answer is usually zero. On the other hand, when I ask the same people how many of their friends have become entrepreneurial successes, the number is much larger. In short, the chance of success is much higher than the chance of a disastrous failure that some people irrationally fear and obsess about.

Interestingly, when I speak with people who've encountered dramatic failures, they discuss their experiences with a sense of pride and satisfaction. They seem fulfilled knowing that they gave it their all, even though things didn't work out the way they had hoped. Many are quite positive about their experiences, often mentioning that their failures were a great learning experience that made them better human beings. No one I've ever met has regretted taking a chance on themselves.

What many non-entrepreneurs seem to fear is the hardship they may face in their entrepreneurial pursuits. We've been conditioned to avoid hardship like the plague and seek jobs that offer the most stability, such as jobs in government, law, medicine, and so on.

But what if we weren't afraid of hardship? Why should life be without hardship in the first place? What if we welcomed hardship as an opportunity for personal growth? Wouldn't life be grander?

Buddhism openly speaks of life being suffering. So, might as well suffer doing something cool! Going to Christian Sunday schools growing up, I read scriptures that instructed us not to fear and that God would be there in times of trial. So, what are we so afraid of?

Takeaway: Embrace hardships and setbacks; they are the building blocks of life's triumph.

19.
Start with a
Mediocre Idea

*"Ideas don't come out fully formed,
they become clearer as you work
on them."*
– Mark Zuckerberg

Wouldn't it be great if we could all come up with that billion-dollar business idea? It would be so much easier to get started if we knew for sure that we had a great idea on hand, wouldn't it?

There are two problems with this wishful thinking. First, such ideas are rare and far between. Moreover, even if you had such an idea, you wouldn't know until you really worked on it. Second, great ideas are not conceived but configured in the process of pivoting from one to another over time.

Unfortunately, some students of mine who really want to be startup entrepreneurs sit still, waiting for the perfect idea that may never materialize. But rather than waiting for years, it's more beneficial to start work with what might seem like an average idea. By working on such an idea, you'll not only hone new skills but also develop the capability to come up with improved ideas in the future.

Moreover, your idea will inevitably evolve and improve. One alumnus from our program launched a startup based on an online B2C game idea. Approximately six years later, when the company was sold, it transformed so dramatically that it became a B2B video delivery technology firm.

An important takeaway here is that without the initial, probably bad, B2C concept and the invaluable customer feedback, the eventual B2B business, obviously good, would never have materialized. Thus, one key to success in this case was simply starting (with a bad idea)!

We know that Facebook today isn't what Mark Zuckerberg initially intended it to be. This begs the question: Was Facebook a good idea when it got started?

It might surprise some that Bank of America, now a leading financial institution in the U.S., was originally called Bank of Italy. It commenced as a modest establishment catering to Italian immigrants in San Francisco. It didn't start with a grand vision or the right business model. The bank underwent a comprehensive metamorphosis from its original vision to the financial powerhouse it is today. It serves as an example of how dramatically companies can evolve from mediocre ideas to great ones.

Takeaway: Start with a decent idea, then pivot to get it right.

20.

Get Started Today – Without Money

"The way to get started is to quit talking and begin doing."
– Walt Disney

A common misconception these days is that you need to raise capital to get started. The reality is that most (well over 90%) of Inc. Magazine's 5000 Fastest Growing companies in any given year did not raise any angel or VC investment (although some secured loans at various stages of their growth).

With some minor exceptions, you can always get started in some way without any capital. If you want to open a bakery, you can start baking in your kitchen until your orders outpace your capacity. If you want to build software, you can entice a few programmers to craft a prototype with persuasive rhetoric and pizza. Any professional service business, like consulting, coaching, or recruiting, can be launched with a phone and a laptop. The key is to start small and demonstrate traction so that you can raise the capital if and when you need it.

Even in capital-intensive industries like hardware, construction, or infrastructure, it's possible to get started with minimal capital—with the right ingenuity. One of my favorite stories is that of Hyundai Heavy Industries, one of the world's largest shipbuilders today.

When the founder wanted to start the company, he needed significant capital to invest in the business's physical infrastructure and a large workforce. Of course, no bank would offer the needed financing since the company had no traction, most notably no customers or purchase orders. However, the company couldn't get any customers because it didn't have the infrastructure or experience of having built ships.

Although the situation might seem insurmountable to most people, the founder did not give up. Miraculously, he was able to secure a purchase order from a major oceanic shipping company without having built a single ship or even having a shipyard for building ships. With the purchase order in hand, he persuaded a prominent British bank to grant his firm a loan to finance the startup.

This story serves as proof that any business can get going without having all the needed funding in place.

Takeaway: You should be able to take your startup quite far without raising funds.

21.
Don't Assume; Market-Test Your Idea(s)

"No business plan survives first contact with customers."
– Steve Blank

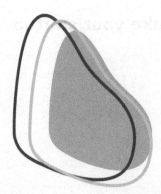

Long before the concepts of "Lean Startup" or "Customer Development Process" were coined, astute entrepreneurs instinctively tested their ideas before committing their precious money or time. It just makes sense to test the feasibility of one's idea early in the process, thereby learning, reducing risk, and, if needed, moving on to the next idea.

The key to the Lean Startup approach to launching a startup is to BUILD a minimal viable product (MVP), get data (MEASURE), and then analyze the data (LEARN) to update one's idea, i.e., hypothesis about what the market wants.*

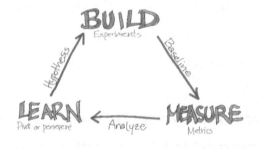

The Lean Startup approach

For instance, when two of our students had the idea for a paper-based whiteboard that students and startup employees could write on, they didn't invest their time and capital right away in the production of the products.

Instead, they set up a website and promoted their whiteboards in several sizes, which they did not yet have. Only when they received tens of thousands of dollars of orders in the ensuing weeks were they assured that there was a healthy market for their products and started getting them manufactured. Writeyboards (https://www.writeyboards.com) has since sold millions of dollars of products.

Similarly, Abstract (https://abstract.co), another LMU startup, cleverly engaged a dozen pilot customers while developing its software solution. By continuously sharing updates and seeking feedback, it ensured that its product would meet actual customer needs. By the time of its official launch, there was little doubt that many companies would find its software valuable.

Takeaway: Validate your idea in the market before committing significant time and resources.

*Ries, E. (2011). *The lean startup: How today's entrepreneurs use continuous innovation to create radically successful businesses.*

03

Launching Your Startup

22.
(Re-) Commit to a Purpose

"The core of entrepreneurship is about making meaning."
– Guy Kawasaki

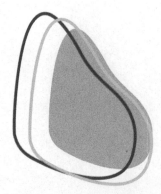

Now that you have a solid understanding of your problem and have arrived at a viable solution, it's time to attain clarity on your startup's core purpose (the reason your company should exist). After some reflection, you might find that your purpose is broader and even more meaningful than solving the core problem at hand. Addressing your original problem is great, but there may be other noble ways you can make the world a better place!

It's tremendously valuable for you and your co-founders to come together to draft a mission statement for the business to ensure that you are all on the same page. A great mission statement authentically represents your team's beliefs and provides ongoing inspiration. An excellent example of a lofty mission statement is Airbnb's:

"Airbnb's mission is to create a world where anyone can belong anywhere, and we are focused on creating an end-to-end travel platform that will handle every part of your trip."

Note that Airbnb's mission is broader and deeper than simply booking a room somewhere. It's also quite inspiring, which is a hallmark of a good mission statement.

Your mission statement can have multiple components. For instance, Ben & Jerry's mission statement includes a product mission, social mission, and economic mission:

- **Product Mission:** *To make, distribute, and sell the finest quality products.*
- **Social Mission:** *To operate the company in a way that actively recognizes the central role that business plays in society by initiating ways to improve the quality of life of local, national, and international communities.*
- **Economic Mission:** *To operate the company on a sound fiscal basis of profitable growth.*

The end objective is to formulate a concise statement that your team commits to and that will serve as a guiding post for your business for years to come.

Takeaway: Write a mission statement that your founding team members agree on and get excited about.

23.

Summon Your Resolve

"The most underrated quality of all is being really determined."
– Sam Altman

Sam Altman, CEO of OpenAI and former president of Y Combinator, argues that determination is the "most important quality of a founder... more important than being smart, having a network, or having a great idea."

Most first-time entrepreneurs have little idea what they are getting themselves into when they launch their companies. They might think, "Since other people do it, how hard can it be?" Well, it's a little like delivering a baby, undergoing basic training in the military, or pulling a wisdom tooth: Many people do these things, but that doesn't make them any easier.

I would say that starting a business and the process of building something from nothing is the hardest thing one can do in business, something that "normal" people would try to avoid. That's why so many of our entrepreneurs in the U.S. are immigrants or children of immigrants who took a huge risk to come to the U.S. and had to summon their resolve to start their lives anew in a foreign country with no money and few friends. Many of the biggest names we know in entrepreneurship are immigrants or their immediate children, e.g., Elon Musk, Steve Jobs, Sergey Brin (Google), Jensen Huang (Nvidia), to name a few.

One of my favorite athletes is Ronnie Lott, a former NFL safety. He was always known for his resolve, toughness, and determination to win. He once broke a finger during a game. Since he was not allowed to play with a broken finger, he convinced the medical staff to cut it off so that he could return to the game! He might have gone overboard with his masculine toughness, and I wouldn't recommend severing any body parts to anyone. However, I have observed a similar level of determination on the part of many entrepreneurs.

As an entrepreneur, you will experience the biggest emotional highs and lows you can imagine. You will fare better if you are mentally prepared for the battle ahead. Studies show that entrepreneurs benefit from prayers, meditation, exercise, and having a support group.

Takeaways: Don't take a knife to a gunfight. Marshal your determination and prepare for an uphill battle.

24.
Convert Your Dreams into (SMART) Goals

"Dreams without goals, are just dreams, and they ultimately fuel disappointment."
– Denzel Washington

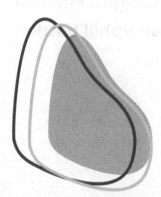

As you embark on your startup journey, it's pivotal to transpose your dreams into goals. You can start with your long-term goals (e.g., to change the world in some way), but you also need to set your short-term goals (such as reaching the next milestone). Whatever your time frame for your goals, it's highly advised to frame them using the "SMART" method.

SMART goals are widely used and considered extremely effective. SMART refers to Specific, Measurable, Achievable, Relevant, and Time-bound. For example, instead of setting a vague long-term goal like "My startup is going to be successful," you can make it more:

- **Specific:** "I aim to be among the largest 3 companies in my industry."
- **Measurable:** "My goal is to reach $50M in revenue."
- **Achievable:** "I plan to expand my partnerships with the leading distribution channels in the industry.:
- **Relevant:** "Being in the top 3 is essential for my company's relevance, economies of scale, and stability."
- **Time-bound:** "I aim to achieve all the goals mentioned above by month 36."

Setting SMART goals can act as a driving force, keeping you motivated and laser-focused. Sharing these goals with your team or peers can offer added accountability. Remember to periodically assess your progress to ensure you remain on track with your SMART goals.

When you set the right goals and achieve them, you will likely be on your way to success. As you set your goals, it's a great time to practice your entrepreneurial mindset and ask yourself: If I were more proactive, what would I do? If I were more innovative, what would I change to my goals? How can I be more resilient in setting and executing my goals?

Anentrepreneurial mindset really comes in handy when things don't work out as planned. You are being proactive insetting goals because no one is telling you to do so. You exercise resilience by being willing to try again. You try new methods when things don't work out, thereby utilizing innovativeness.

Takeaway: Turn your dreams into SMART goals to ensure they come true.

25.

Craft a Compelling Value Proposition

"Your product might be amazing. But without a succinct value proposition, your customers may never know why."
– Adam Enfroy

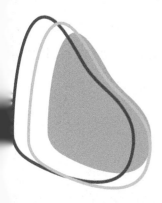

It might seem easy to some folks, but many entrepreneurs have difficulty explaining what makes their startup special – the essence of a value proposition. A value proposition is a succinct statement that clearly defines what a business offers and how it stands out from competitors, often articulated in just a few sentences.

A well-crafted value proposition is crucial as it clearly and succinctly informs potential customers of the advantages they would receive by choosing your business over others. This statement should be highlighted on your company website and be central to your pitches when seeking to close a sale.

There are a couple of reasons why entrepreneurs have difficulty with their value proposition. First, it's hard to know what sets you apart until you've spoken to many customers and learned what they (or a segment of them) truly value. You may need to pivot and adjust your solution based on customer feedback. Second, it's not easy to express your company's strengths in a few sentences when you are so emotionally invested. Few words don't seem to do your idea justice.

However, once you do have a clear understanding of where your business stands, you should make an effort to formulate an exciting and succinct value proposition statement.

Steve Blank, one of the most renowned entrepreneurship professors today, proposes this structure, "We help (X) do (Y) by doing (Z)," to craft a value proposition.

For example: "We help our local customers satisfy their sweet tooth by providing them with premium natural ice cream in a community-focused space."

For a company like Less Accounting Software, its value proposition might be: "We help entrepreneurs who dislike accounting effectively manage their businesses with our simple software." Of course, you could make it even more to the point: "Simple accounting software for entrepreneurs who dislike accounting."

Takeaway: Make sure to always have a compelling value proposition statement at your disposal.

26.
Figure Out
(and Change)
Your Business Model

*"A startup is a temporary
organization in search of a
business model."*
– Steve Blank

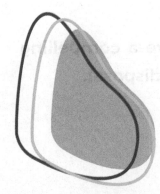

A business model defines how a company creates value for itself while delivering products and services to its customers. In simpler terms, it's the strategy a company uses to earn a profit.

It's standard practice today to use the Business Model Canvas to analyze and strategize a firm's business model. Note that the business model consists of important building blocks such as the right value proposition, customer relationships, partners, resources, activities, target audience, marketing channels, cost drivers, and revenue streams.

Continually adapt and test new strategies until you land on the right business model. When you find the correct one, your business should be positioned to grow and yield profits. On the other hand, a lack of growth and profitability indicates that you have not yet found the right business model for your business.

The Business Model Canvas allows you to visualize the evolution of your business model as your strategies change. For instance, consider how a small construction business might shift from catering to individual homeowners to serving government agencies. Such a transition would involve modifying various elements of the business model, such as their approach to customer relationships or marketing channels (e.g., moving from Yelp reviews to writing formal proposals).

Here is a suggestion: Fill out a Business Model Canvas based on your current business. Over time, highlight and observe the adjustments as they occur. It's quite educational to see how your business model evolves.

Takeaway: Fill out your Business Model Canvas to visualize and fully grasp all the elements of your business model.

27.
Transform Yourself into a Prolific Marketer

"The business enterprise has two, and only two, basic functions: marketing and innovation. Marketing and innovation produce results; all the rest are costs."

– Peter Drucker

For many budding entrepreneurs, the reality can be harsh. They introduce a fantastic product or service that customers can benefit from, only to find few takers! Having fallen in love with their innovation, many entrepreneurs (especially engineer types like me) don't realize the importance of marketing (or selling). It turns out that no product sells itself.

As Professor Peter Drucker, a leading scholar in the field of management, used to emphasize, marketing and innovation are the two most paramount functions of any business. Interestingly, he placed marketing ahead of innovation in his statement above.

I can't overstate the significance of marketing for startups. Marketing is not just advertising; it's a lot more. It encompasses developing a deep insight into your customers' mindset, strategizing on how best to position the startup's offerings to attract early adopters, discovering what sales channels are most effective, identifying the customer segments for which your offerings are most competitive, fine-tuning the messaging, etc. Good marketing can make a huge difference in the trajectory of a startup.

I've seen a former LMU student's startup become a market leader with an average product supported by great marketing (that included beautiful packaging and exceptional online marketing skills).

On the other hand, many of the entrepreneurs I've met over the years did not appreciate the importance of marketing and did not engage in it on an ongoing basis. In fact, I've known dozens of construction and professional service entrepreneurs being reluctant to engage in marketing and selling activities. Some called on customers only when they had downtime between projects. The problem is that these downtimes often became really long, thereby reducing the firm's revenues and growth potential.

Eventually, these firms learned to discipline themselves to take scheduled breaks (e.g., every Tuesday and Thursday afternoon) from their projects to visit with past and prospective customers to acquire projects and schedule them throughout the year. This simple change also allowed many of our firms to prepare for and achieve growth.

Takeaway: Make marketing a priority, not an afterthought.

28. Seek and Be Receptive to Advice

"Don't be the smartest person in the room; hang out with people smarter than you."
– Michael Dell

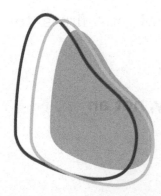

Many young entrepreneurs mistakenly associate confidence and self-belief with dismissing outside advice. When seasoned entrepreneurs advise that you should not always listen to others, they mean that you should ignore certain critics who are probably wrong or might not have your best interests at heart. They are likely not suggesting that you should be closed to feedback and become uncoachable.

While blindly accepting other people's suggestions is certainly not recommended, heeding insights from seasoned experts can be very beneficial. Studies also show that establishing an advisory board can positively benefit startups.

No one should be so overconfident as to feel that only they know the answers. Some of the most successful entrepreneurs I've met are both humble and inquisitive people. For example, Paul Orfalea, founder of Kinko's (which sold for $2.4 billion) and a standout instructor at LMU, often approaches me with questions. He exudes natural curiosity, humility, and an eagerness to learn from others' views.

Some of the worst entrepreneurs I've met were those who refused to listen to other people's opinions.
I actually understand why they acted that way.

It's not that they were always overconfident individuals. They reached a certain level of success by ignoring the naysayers. So, it's reasonable (though still not wise) to believe that they should keep going against the advice of others.

Investors are particularly sensitive about the "coachability" of entrepreneurs. Disagreements are acceptable, but dismissing advice or reacting poorly to constructive feedback is seen as a critical red flag to venture capitalists.

In summary, entrepreneurs need to be confident and believe in themselves, but it's equally important for entrepreneurs to strike a balance between self-confidence and humility. They need to understand that there's always something new to learn and that great ideas can come from others.

Takeaway: Be receptive to sound advice, while remaining humble and coachable.

*Choi, D.Y. & Stack, M. (2005). Who adds value to ventures? Understanding the roles and relative contributions of key advisors in high-technology startups. *Journal of Entrepreneurial Finance.*

29.
Build the Best Team That You Can

"The best thing I ever created was a team."
– Steve Jobs

One of the most important aspects of starting a company is selecting your co-founder(s) and initial team members. What would Steve Jobs have achieved without his Apple co-founder Steve Wozniak, the skilled engineer who actually built the technologies they envisioned? Similarly, Bill Gates had Paul Allen; the older, more connected, and the more established of the duo.

So, how does one identify an exceptional team member? While it would be ideal if your favorite picnic companion were also the perfect business partner, this is seldom the case. You can't just pick your best friend(s) because it's vital to ensure that your skill sets are complementary. This often means partnering with someone who possesses different expertise, studied a different major in college, and perhaps even approaches work differently. But it's not enough for your co-founders' skills to simply complement yours; they should also be real experts in their field.

This is why finding the right person(s) requires significant effort, and you may not get it right the first time. I once befriended a young (and highly successful) entrepreneur was always obsessed with finding talented co-founders. He would attend social events (parties!) always on the lookout for talented engineers and marketers (rather than dates) he could recruit for his current and next startups.

Building a harmonious relationship with co-founders can be extremely challenging. I once posed the following question to a venture capitalist I respected: "Why is it that we often start companies with our closest friends, only to discover that we can't work effectively together?" He replied, "Because we don't really know our friends."

He explained that, while it's easy to get along with friends at school, picnics, and parties, working side by side on a daily basis is an entirely different dynamic.

While it's super important to build your team with the most talented individuals you can find, it's equally critical to bring in people who buy into your mission, values, and plan, and who have a great attitude about work and life. My experience has been that attitude trumps IQ and experience any day.

Takeaway: Invest time and effort to assemble the best possible team.

30.
Assume that You are a Bad Leader

"Leaders are made rather than born."
– Warren Bennis

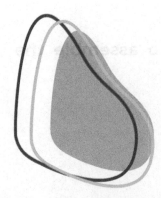

When I ask my students in my classes if they are good at mathematics, only a few hands go up. On the other hand, when I ask my students if they have good leadership skills, almost everyone raises their hands.

Chances are that most of my students (and most people)overestimate their leadership skills. Everyone knows whether they are good or bad in mathematics or accounting. Grades can serve as an indicator of competence in these areas. However, few people are aware of their inadequate people skills. I recall a Gallup poll once reporting that only about 10% of individuals possess the innate talent to become effective leaders.

I have encountered startup CEOs unaware of the importance of regular communication with their teams. Most managers don't even know the very basics of leadership. Unfortunately, most entrepreneurs (and even corporate executives) never receive a minute of leadership training. Yet, just like my students, most startup CEOs remain confident about their leadership skills.

The startup CEOs whom I am most concerned about are those who never had a boss before. These folks never had a chance to learn at least what not to do as a boss. Some CEOs I met mistakenly believed that leadership was all about dictating to people what to do. Others thought that they were good bosses because they were excessively nice and agreeable. The reality is that some did not have enough exposure to good leaders or teams to grasp the nuances of leadership and its significant impact on an organization.

It's a good idea to assumethat you have a lot to learn about leadership. Commit to cultivating your leadership skills. Each day presentsan opportunity to lead more effectively. Dive into books, engage in lectures, and seek wisdom from those with more experience.

Takeaway: Prioritize enhancing your leadership competence – its significance cannot be overstated.

31.
Let Your Co-Founders Earn Their Ownership

"A man is usually more careful of his money than he is of his principles."
– Ralph Waldo Emerson

I purposely did not include financial or legal advice in this book, but this particular mistake among first-time founders is so common that I felt compelled to discuss it here.

Imagine you get together with your good friends, brainstorm a great business idea, and decide to start a company together. So far so good. A common detrimental mistake that follows is that you and your co-founders sign a legally binding agreement that divides up the ownership pie (often equally), only to find out a few months later that one or more of your co-founders have accepted jobs elsewhere with higher pay and less risk.

The problem now is that a significant portion of the company is owned by friends who are no longer with the business. Then, you and the remaining committed co-founders learn that your departed "friends," despite having abandoned you, are reluctant to give up their ownership stakes. Basically, they want to make money doing nothing on the back of years of your blood and sweat. Surprisingly, they feel no guilt whatsoever.

This situation is detrimental for you and all those still dedicated to the business also because it renders the company less appealing to potential investors.

No investor wants to finance a company whose ownership is taken up by people not working in the business.

What happens next? You find yourself borrowing money from your parents to buy out your former friends (or enemies), compensating them for having done nothing.

To circumvent this issue, in the first place I would advise:

1. Collaborate only with serious individuals
2. Give ownership to only those committing to the startup.
3. To achieve #2, implement a vesting schedule for all shares allocated to co-founders and employees. This means everyone needs to earn ownership over 3 or 4 years, thereby limiting ownership by people who leave the company.
4. Establish an agreed-upon mechanism for remaining team members to purchase shares from departing members.

Takeaway: Set up a vesting schedule for everyone's ownership in your startup.

32.
Go for Speed
(and Quick Traction)

"I have been impressed with the
urgency of doing. Knowing is not
enough. We must apply. Being willing
is not enough. We must do."
– Leonardo da Vinci

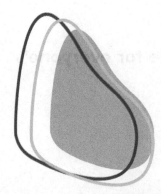

There's a reason the first two questions on the television show Shark Tank usually are, "What are your sales?" and "How long have you been in business?" Investors are keen to gauge the traction a startup has garnered and the pace of its achievements. These factors reflect both the merit of the idea and the proficiency of the involved entrepreneur(s).

When you start a company, you have to gain traction and do it *quickly*. The clock starts ticking the moment you launch. Not only is timely traction personally satisfying, but it also becomes the basis for how the world views and judges you.

When a startup gains traction, a myriad of opportunities arise. Seasoned managers and engineers become eager to join, while prominent lawyers and advisors offer their assistance at discounted rates. Investors start making time to meet with you. Without timely traction, none of those mentioned above happen.

The most important measures of traction are financial: revenue and profit. Initially, you might need to settle for other metrics like the number of customers or downloads. Whatever your initial goals are, you must utilize every conventional and unconventional method to achieve them. You cannot work 8-hour days, take frequent vacations, or let your suppliers work at their regular speeds.

Given that the Empire State Building was built in just about 13 months, why should your small business take longer to launch? If you think about it, many of the greatest achievements in human history and entrepreneurship, whether it's the Great Pyramids or the iPhone, were accomplished at remarkable speeds.

Speedy product deployment also increases the likelihood of achieving product-market fit and gaining a competitive advantage. If you find that your startup is progressing slowly, you may need to examine your own leadership and project management skills. You and your team might be lacking some necessary expertise or connections. At a minimum, make sure that you are not being the bottleneck with slow and poor decision-making.

Takeaway: Work with urgency to secure traction and build momentum.

04

Growing Your Startup

33.
Know Your Numbers!

"The sin that I see most often and the disasters that occur in the Shark Tank is if you don't know your numbers. You tend to get killed."
– Kevin O'Leary

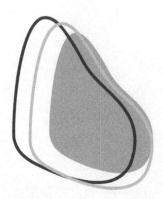

Many of our most visionary and creative entrepreneurs are not entirely comfortable with numbers. Richard Branson, founder of Virgin, often jokes about getting "revenue" and "profit" mixed up. While he may be playing up his persona as a fun and relatable figure, the underlying message is clear.

Entrepreneurs don't need to be world-class accountants, but understanding numbers is crucial for achieving financial success. You also want to avoid embarrassment on Shark Tank when Kevin O'Leary and Mark Cuban question you about your financials and other metrics.

Even if you find accounting and finance challenging (those courses are supposed to be challenging), that's not an excuse for not mastering your business' finances. You can't just say that you are "bad with numbers". I often get the "I am not good with numbers" excuse from my students. I find that excuse to be nonsensical, something that is correctable with a few hours of effort.

It's essential to familiarize oneself with the key terms and not be intimidated by them. There is reason to fear: the mathematics needed for business seldom exceeds the 7th-grade level.

Thus, anyone with a middle school education should be capable of handling their company's finances. Simply put, no valid reason for not understanding one's numbers. All it takes is a bit of time and effort.

Key accounting terms you should be comfortable with include:
- Revenue (monthly (MRR), annual (ARR))
- Cost of Goods/Cost of Sales
- General & Administrative (G&A)
- Operating Profit & Net Profit
- Cash Balance & Cash Flow
- Burn Rate
- Accounts Receivable/Payable

Moreover, it's important to know your:
- Customer Acquisition Cost (CAC)
- Lifetime Value of Customers (LTV)

You can google or ask ChatGPT for these terms when you forget. Again remember, business isn't rocket science, but you have to keep score. As Dick Schulze, founder and former CEO of Best Buy often says, "The difference between an amateur and professional is that the professional keeps score."

Takeaway: Overcome your fear of numbers and stay on top of your finances.

34.
Don't Limit Yourself to Conventional Funding

"When one door of happiness closes, another opens; but often we look so long at the closed door that we do not see the one which has been opened for us."
– Helen Keller

The most common question I get from entrepreneurs is "How do I raise the funds I need for my startup?"

Supposedly, when Steve Jobs started Apple, he went to a bank and asked for a loan. That didn't go well since banks didn't give out loans for tech startups. They still don't. Fortunately for Jobs, alternative funding sources were emerging: angel investing and venture capital. He was able to take advantage of them.

Even today, entrepreneurs need to be open to various financing sources and evaluate which are the right ones for their businesses. Some entrepreneurs focus solely on traditional financing sources, such as large banks and famous VC firms. However, neither of these are likely sources of capital for most startups. Most entrepreneurs don't qualify for conventional loans due to the nature of their businesses or their imperfect credit histories. The vast majority of small businesses don't meet the growth rate criteria for venture capital.

Nevertheless, most businesses have a suitable financing option or two; it's a matter of finding them. For instance, Kickstarter might be the ideal choice for early-stage startups developing creative films or product ideas. Kiva is an excellent crowdfunding platform for receiving micro-loans.

Various crowdfunding platforms cater to different types of businesses, e.g., Ecocrowdto startups focused on sustainability. If you keep getting rejections, it might be that you haven't discovered the right funding sources yet. Additionally, consider exploring community banks or CDFIs, which often provide more accessible loan and even some equity funding.

One of the best sources of financing can be your corporate client. If you can get all or a portion of your sales paid upfront, you may not need to raise capital. I know of an engineering firm that was able to build its prototype without raising capital *and* deliver the solution to its customer because the customer paid upfront. Or, if you can at least receive a purchase order from a credible buyer, you can qualify for a loan or an angel investment more easily.

It's also possible that you happen to run a business for which there simply is no good funding and that you have no choice but to "bootstrap" and grow slowly by getting one customer at a time. That's hard, but it's nothing to get discouraged about. Financing your business through operations is an old-fashioned yet proven method. Many of today's large businesses have used this slow and steady approach for their growth.

Takeaway: Harness your entrepreneurial hustle to find the right financing for your business.

35.
Get to Know Your Investors

"Your network is your net worth."
– Porter Gale

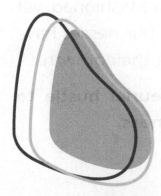

Business gets easier (somewhat) when you have an established professional network, and your local VCs, bankers, and corporate partners think highly of you. That's one reason experienced entrepreneurs, those on their second and third startups, often find traction more quickly.

As a new, budding entrepreneur, you won't have a personal relationship with many investors yet. So, you have to be a little more diligent and strategic. Rule of thumb: Most investors or bankers won't finance your business immediately, no matter how good of a first impression you make. They will want to get to know you and learn how good you are as a businessperson, all of which takes time.

Some of the savvy first-time entrepreneurs I've known who have successfully cultivated relationships with local investors or bankers quickly have the following in common: They attended various industry / investor / demo day events, and repeatedly met with angels, VCs, and bankers early in their startup journey. These slick entrepreneurs didn't ask the investors for funding immediately (their startups weren't ready anyway) but shared what they were working on.

When these entrepreneurs ran into the investors again at an event, they greeted them with a smile and updated them on the milestones achieved since their last conversation. Before long, the entrepreneurs and investors began feeling comfortable with each other, sparking trust and familiarity in the process.

I once advised a biotech entrepreneur who made sure to keep in touch with a senior executive from a mid-sized bank. He and I met together with the banker every few months without exactly knowing when we might use his services. A few years down the line, when the startup required a significant loan to acquire another company, the bank promptly approved the request.

This financial boost played a pivotal role in the startup's dramatic expansion. A couple of years later, when the U.S. Federal Government offered financial assistance to businesses affected due to the hardship caused by COVID-19, the bank worked swiftly to support the biotech company. The biotech firm survived and prospered over the next few years eventually resulting in a remarkably profitable sale.

Takeaway: Make it a point to introduce yourself to bankers and investors today.

36.
Raise Money When You Don't Need It

"The best time to ask for money is when you don't need it."
– Mark Cuban

It's ironic but true. When your business is thriving and you don't need capital, it seems that every bank reaches out to you eagerly to discuss its latest loan offerings. In contrast, when you are in dire need of financing, no bank appears interested in meeting with you. Basically, the same thing happens with venture capitalists.

So, the best time to raise money is when things are progressing nicely and, therefore, you aren't desperate for financing. When business is good, raising capital is relatively easy. You point to your strong past financial performance, and the process is quite straightforward.

Even if you've raised some capital not too long ago, you should raise the next round while you still have plenty of capital to last a while. You will be and appear relaxed and confident, and that will make you a more attractive candidate for investment. You will also get better terms.

Naturally, there could be times when you find yourself urgently needing an investment to keep your business afloat. It's usually hard to fool investors because many of them have a knack for discerning the desperate financial position you're in.

However, even in these dire circumstances, it's crucial to exude confidence and present an optimistic outlook for your startup's future to financiers.

Once you've decided to seek capital, it's wise to engage in discussions with several entities simultaneously. This ensures don't get cornered into having limited options. It's difficult to say "No" to an offer if it's the only one you have, especially if you invested months of your time working on the deal, even if the deal is quite unfavorable for you.

Takeaway: Position yourself in the best possible situation for raising capital.

37.
Free-Up Your Time

*"Your most important task as a
leader is to teach people how to
think and ask the right questions so
that the world doesn't go to hell if
you take a day off."*
– Jeff Bezos

For the majority of entrepreneurs, the prevailing cause of their firms' stunted growth is their "lack of time".* This is not surprising. Most of them work long hours each day, six or seven days a week, and many cannot find the additional time or energy that could take their business to the next level.

Most of them know conceptually that they need to allocate their time more effectively - to the tasks they are great at and directly contribute to business growth. For instance, most know that they should spend less time on menial office management tasks and focus on activities that really matter, e.g., meeting with customers or new business partners. However, most early-stage business owners don't feel that they have the funds to hire the people to support the business, and, of course, the business owners don't have the funds because they cannot spend enough time growing the business.

Fortunately, there are options. For example, if you can't afford an administrative assistant, there are "virtual assistants" who can help with many of your time-consuming tasks at less than half of the price. If managing your schedule becomes overwhelming, there are both free and cost-effective software tools available. If managing social media consumes too much of your time, consider employing a motivated college student or a remote worker, which can be surprisingly economical.

I've seen entrepreneurs hire assistants and then fire them only a few weeks later because the new hires can't do the work as efficiently as they can. These entrepreneurs need to have a little more patience and let their new hires develop into their roles.

As a founder and leader, you need to delegate and be freed up to focus on your company's most important tasks. Your eventual objective should be to build an internal system that allows your business to operate smoothly without your constant presence. Your goal is to work "on" your business, not "in" your business. Remember, you are working on creating a thriving company, not your job.

Takeaway: Prioritize and delegate to focus on activities that truly drive business growth.

*Forbes (2022; Jan 28). *Ways to navigate the first stage of small business growth.*

38.
Build a Positive Culture in Your Organization

"Culture eats strategy for breakfast."
– Peter Drucker

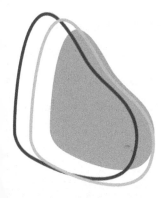

You can step into a small bakery and immediately sense the firm's culture. A good culture is often reflected in the employees' motivation, attitude, and the quality of service they provide, all of which foster customer loyalty and contribute to business success. Whether positive or negative, a culture is hard to miss. A good culture is rarely created by chance; it is intentionally crafted.

Unfortunately, many entrepreneurs mistakenly think that organizational culture is something that only large corporations should worry about. However, every business, regardless of its size, inherently has a culture that can make a huge difference in the company's performance.

Building a great culture often begins with simple actions such as sharing your objectives with your team, treating them with respect, fostering open communication, and leading by example. Contrary to what some may think, culture building does not require much money at all.

I'm acquainted with a wonderful entrepreneur in the construction sector who adeptly cultivated a positive culture by ensuring that his workers had ample water on-site, celebrating their birthdays, and holding Hawaiian shirt days on Fridays.

These simple and cost-effective actions paved the way for the company's vibrant culture with committed employees, which led to stellar operational performance and eventual financial success. Of course, it helped that the founder was a good leader who constantly visited construction sites to check up on the quality of the work and the condition of his employees.

Establishing a culture is an investment that can yield substantial returns. Employees who feel valued and understand the effort expected of them deliver improved performance, which often leads to savings and higher profits.

Takeaway: Dedicate a few moments daily to nurture a vibrant work culture.

*Barney, J. B. (1986). Organizational culture: can it be a source of sustained competitive advantage? *Academy of Management Review*, 11(3), 656-665.

39.
Don't Be a
Cheapskate

*"Don't be penny wise, and
pound foolish."*
– Benjamin Franklin

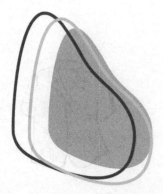

Business is all about maximizing profit, or is it?

Maybe. But it's also more complicated than that. Even if we believed in the statement above, our decision would depend on the time horizon. We would want to avoid the mistake of maximizing short-term profits at the expense of much larger earning potential in the future.

I sometimes overhear entrepreneurs as well as corporate executives boasting about what a great deal they got by underpaying a vendor or contractor. I am not sure why one would brag about shortchanging someone from earning a living. But more importantly, such one-sided business practices may be bad for your company in the long run.

Certainly, there may be situations when you just go for the lowest cost, but, at minimum, you need to treat your important business partners with more care and respect. They need to be able to sustain their operation to ensure their continued survival and high-quality service. A good long-term relationship can really benefit your business, and it's also the right thing to do.

Mr. Ewing Kauffman, the esteemed founder of the Kauffman Foundation, a national organization promoting entrepreneurship, used to run an international life science firm. On one occasion, his CFO returned from a trip to Germany, proud of his hard negotiation tactics that squeezed one of their key suppliers. Concerned about how little profit the supplier was going to make, Mr. Kauffman instructed his CFO to return to Germany and offer their supplier better terms.

A few years later, when the market for the supplier's products was in significant demand, Mr. Kauffman's company was prioritized over others, and therefore was able to receive a steady supply and maintain its growth trajectory. This story is a testament to the value of fostering good relationships with one's business partners.

While profitability is vital, if your business model relies on constantly squeezing your employees or partners, it might be time to reconsider your approach. Foster solid relationships with all key stakeholders, from vendors to employees and customers.

Takeaway: Build great relationships with the people you do business with.

40.
Run Your Company with Decency

"Values are like fingerprints...you leave them all over everything you do."
– Elvis Presley

There is a huge misunderstanding about business among some people – that you have to be dishonest and cruel to succeed! While such (mis-)behaviors can work for some in the short term, they won't work in the long run and certainly won't make running a business fun or rewarding. There is a reason why so many successful businesspeople are upstanding citizens who are honest and fair, and at times, incredibly generous.

Remember your business's mission and that business can be a force for good as well as a vehicle for making a difference. You started (or are starting) your business to make the world a better place in some way. Your business may or may not succeed in the end, but you can affect people's lives and the planet each day that you are in business.

Also, remember that so many entrepreneurs have already shown the way. Look at firms like Newman's Own, Patagonia, Interface, and The Body Shop that have already demonstrated that you can be profitable as well as responsible.

I had the privilege of advising a college friend's software company, which was often ranked as one of the best small businesses to work for.

One of the first software applications that the company built was for its internal use: At 11 am, a box would pop up on every employee's computer screen asking them which of the lunch menu items of the day they preferred. At noon, all employees would gather in the company's kitchen to share a meal and forge their friendships. The company's refrigerator was always stacked with unlimited amounts of soft drinks as well as adult beverages.

My friend (CEO) loved his employees like family, and they loved him back. He gave them ownership in an overly generous manner, but they paid him back with a profitable exit when a major private equity firm eventually acquired the company. Equally important for him, he has the peace of mind of knowing that he did his very best to take care of his people.

Some say, "Business is business." Remember, your business is also a reflection of who you are and what you stand for.

Takeaway: Build the kind of organization that you would like your children to work for.

41.

Scale - Go for Growth

"The biggest risk is not taking any risk. In a world that is changing quickly, the only strategy that is guaranteed to fail is not taking risks."
– Mark Zuckerberg

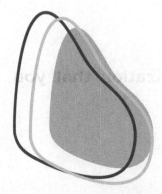

Growing a company from nothing to something is incredibly difficult, perhaps one of the toughest tasks in business. Trying to create momentum for a new startup can feel like pushing a boulder uphill.

However, once your business model is finally solidified and things are generally clicking, it's time to scale your business. Scaling can take the form of boosting your advertising spend, securing a second or third location, and enlarging your sales and operations team, among others. It's an opportunity to apply your proven formula for success, such as specific operational processes or marketing strategies, on a grander scale.

Typically, scaling involves accessing additional financial resources, like securing a more substantial line of credit, obtaining a business loan, or even attracting venture capital or private equity investment. Scaling also involves building a larger management team, often recruiting people with extensive expertise and experience.

It's noteworthy that some firms become overly cautious when they start to see profits. Many do not want to jeopardize what they just accomplished.

Of course, it's totally acceptable to grow slowly if more responsibilities are not something you want to take on. Perhaps you want to turn your business into a multi-generational family business and don't want to take on additional investors. However, not growing can also pose existential and financial risks in the future, and I have seen entrepreneurs later regret not scaling when they could have.

Reid Hoffman, the co-founder of LinkedIn, is in favor of growth. He suggests that firms should have no hesitation about pursuing growth. He does recommend that firms learn from mistakes and iterate quickly to ensure profitable growth.*

Of course, it's up to the entrepreneur to decide whether or not to grow and how. However, I hope that entrepreneurs don't limit themselves just because of their fears or misconceptions about debt or their lack of familiarity with the various growth options.

Takeaway: Prepare to scale your business and be sure to know all your strategic options.

*Hoffman, R. (2021) *Masters of Scale: Surprising Truths from the World's Most Successful Entrepreneurs.*

42.
Don't Waste Time Thinking About an Exit

"The best investment the founders can make in their startup is to go about their own business and think about growth."
– Paul Graham

When you meet investors, they often inquire about your eventual "exit strategy", even if it has been only a few months since you launched your startup.

Navigating investor expectations can be tricky. Some may raise eyebrows if you seem too keen on selling. It's understandable since you should be focused on building a great company. At the same time, some investors might be apprehensive if you appear unwilling to consider a sale even some years later. Some investors get wary if you mention the word "IPO" (which stands for initial public offering, which expresses your intention to run a publicly traded firm) because very few companies grow large enough to go public, and even if yours could, it might take too long.

The best way to address this is to say: "For now, we are focused on growing our company, but we will always be open to your advice."

It's generally advised not to sell too early. Larger businesses sell at a disproportionately higher price. A $1M revenue might sell for 2 times revenue, but a similar firm with $10M revenue might sell for 5 times revenue. So, it often makes sense to be patient and just focus on growth for a number of years.

Thus, there is no need to spend much time thinking about selling in the earlier years. Your focus should be on building a great company.

Interestingly, as your business grows, you'll be surprised by the number of bankers, consultants, and competitors reaching out with exit/acquisition-related questions. In fact, a whole industry exists, that is keen to present you with a wide range of potential selling opportunities.

You might say "What about Youtube? They were acquired within 15 months of starting for more than a billion dollars?" They exited in no time at all! Well, there are always exceptions to the general rule. You can also win the lottery, and people do it every day. But you can't design a plan based on the assumption that you will get super lucky someday. So, in your initial years, sit tight and focus on growth.

Takeaway: Focus on growing your business – you will have plenty of opportunities to sell.

05

Continue Your
Personal Growth

43.

Invest in Your Health and Fitness

"A person who has health has hope, and a person who has hope has everything."
– Arabian Proverb

One of the best ways to prepare for and deal with the bumpy ride of entrepreneurship is to invest in health. With health, I don't mean just not being sick. To succeed as an entrepreneur or in any demanding profession, it helps a great deal to be ultra-healthy, i.e., energetic and fit.

A well-known academic study on the relationship between entrepreneurship and fitness published in the Journal of Small Business Management indicates that entrepreneurs who exercised more often had businesses with higher revenues. Long-distance running was the exercise that made the biggest difference. It makes sense considering that the entrepreneurial journey is very much a "marathon", requiring stamina over an extended period of time. I find that, among the male entrepreneurs around me, an unusually high percentage of them engage in weight-lifting and other strength exercises.

Several books by Dr. Daniel G. Amen, an authority on brain health, reveal that basically the same foods and exercises that are good for the body are also good for the brain.** In terms of exercises, Dr. Amen strongly recommends racket sports and strength exercises.

He emphasizes that muscle-building exercises like weightlifting are great for maintaining a high level of brain function. In summary, maintaining a healthy body helps you keep a sharp mind, which together has a huge impact on one's business performance.

Based on my observations of my former students working in large corporations, it's again the fit individuals who appear to be on the fast track to top management. I have also noticed that of the small business owners I have coached, it's the entrepreneurs with high energy levels who secure large contracts from governments and corporations. So, fitness might be something that is advantageous regardless of where you end up working.

One corporate executive explained to me: "When I see an employee or a potential business partner who is fit or has obviously been pumping iron, I don't think "this person is wasting too much time exercising." I think 'this person is disciplined and therefore will deliver on the work they promised.'" I don't know if the belief above is widely held among other corporate executives or whether it's fair to even think like he did. It certainly doesn't sound fair when you think about so many people suffering from health conditions or even diseases.

However, for enterprising young people who are healthy, the possibility that one's fitness may be perceived as a sign of professionalism may offer additional motivation to stay healthy and exercise on a regular basis. It's easy to blame one's busy schedule for not exercising, but most people can find 20 minutes here and there which can make a difference in the long run. Research is clear: Taking care of your health does more than make you look and feel like a million dollars.

Takeaway: Invest in your health and fitness to increase the chance of your success.

*Michael G. Goldsby, Donald F. Kuratko & James W. Bishop (2005) Entrepreneurship and Fitness: An Examination of Rigorous Exercise and Goal Attainment among Small Business Owners, *Journal of Small Business Management*, 43:1, 78-92.

**Amen, D. G. (2006). *Making a good brain great: The Amen clinic program for achieving and sustaining optimal mental performance.* Harmony.

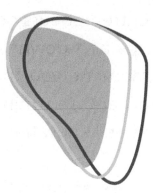

44.

Maintain Your Sanity

"Do not pray for an easy life, pray for the strength to endure a difficult one."
– Bruce Lee

Entrepreneurs go through some incredible emotional ups and downs – sometimes on the same day. One moment, you think you are on your way to a billion dollars. Ten minutes later, you feel like the biggest loser. I know this feeling all too well.

These emotional roller coasters are difficult to handle even when things are going well overall. Imagine your business is on a positive trajectory and on its way to success. Even then, the weekly dramatic ups and downs are hard to deal with. They can affect one's psychological health, and many entrepreneurs end up falling into depression or developing addictive habits. When one's business has more downs than ups for some time, it can get really challenging.

There are ways to deal with this. Common strategies include:

1. Don't let minor setbacks drag you down. Find comforts in quotes like: "Promise yourself to be so strong that nothing can disturb your peace of mind... to be too large for worry, too noble for anger, too strong for fear, and too happy to permit the presence of trouble" (Christian D. Larson quote).

2. Celebrate small wins: Focused on work, many entrepreneurs forget to have fun even when good things happen. Having celebrations for small wins with your co-founders and employees helps prolong the happy moments.

3. Meditation: Many of my former students have benefited from meditation, yoga, and of course, prayer. Academic research indicates that many people develop philosophical or religious approaches to dealing with the swings of their business situations.

4. Build a support group: Psychological studies have also shown that support groups (e.g., family and friends) can help entrepreneurs stay resilient toward their goals.

You should try whatever method works for you, but one thing is for sure: You cannot let the ups and downs of your business uncontrollably swing your emotions. Nobody said that changing the world would be easy. Make sure to work on your emotional strengths to endure the demands of your entrepreneurial journey.

Takeaway: Don't let the ups and downs of your business affect your mental health.

A Day In The Life As An Entrepreneur

"I'm good. I don't know why I get so down on myself"

"Wait a second. My life is great."

"Give up the good for the great!"

"ITS WORKING!"

"I'm excited"

"I messed up"

"Ugh! This hard"

"I was wrong. I suck!"

"I think I'm going bankrupt"

Created by Derek Halpern

45.
Don't be Shy About Making Money

"May you have all the happiness and luck that life can hold, and at the end of your rainbows, may you find a pot of gold."
– Irish Blessing

I often ask my undergraduate students in class the question: "Does anyone want to make money?" Usually, only a few raise their hands. Typically, one or more students respond with statements like, "My goal in life isn't to make money." Then, I clarified myself by saying, "I never asked if that's your only goal. Just asking if you want to make a lot of money or just have a little bit of it." At this time, I usually see about a quarter to a third of my students being still reluctant to raise their hands. To a certain extent, I am proud of these students for being idealistic, as young people should be. I also understand that it may also be years of catholic education that caused me to be overly hesitant about wanting money.

Ironically, at my university, I see another group of students, those who like to show off their super-fancy cars that their parents bought for them. It's as if they are trying to send the message, "Look at me, I am rich and spoiled. I have parents who waste money on me. I am really bad with money too." I can see that these students enjoy having and flaunting money. I personally don't quite understand why people proudly show off their parents' money – something they had no hand in earning.

Of course, once you've made your own money through legitimate methods, even if you've been taught that money is the root of all evil, you should be proud of your achievement. I don't think anything is wrong with wanting or making much of it. And newsflash: Money is not necessarily evil.

How you make your money and what you spend it on are the important questions. Yes, you should make money in the right way (like Google's unofficial motto, "Don't be evil"). Set a standard for yourself in terms of what business you get yourself into how you treat people, and how you minimize your environmental footprint.

I personally couldn't have worked for companies that produced tobacco, weapons, coal, certain foods and drinks, etc., or mistreated customers. That's why I chose education, foods (salad dressing), medical diagnostics, and software.

Everyone wants good people to win – make sure that you are someone we can cheer for.

Takeaway: Pick the right business and business model – and then make all the money you can.

46.
Share Your Success Secrets with Others

"If I have seen further, it is by standing on the shoulders of giants."

– Isaac Newton

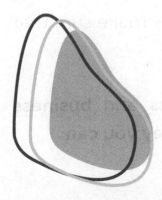

As the famous African proverb goes, "It takes a village to raise a child." I've seen firsthand how truthful the statement is. It takes parents, relatives, teachers, coaches, neighbors, various organizations, volunteers, and even kind strangers to safely and properly develop a child into an adolescent and eventually an adult.

I think most people would agree that it also takes an entire village to develop one successful entrepreneur or business. In the U.S., it's amazing how so many people give their time and resources to struggling entrepreneurs with no strings attached. Many of today's successful entrepreneurs would never have had a chance without such supporters. These supporters include the parents who empty their savings for their kids' ideas, the first customer who gives the startup a chance, the angel investor who believes in the struggling entrepreneur, as well as other official or unofficial advisors who give more of their time than financially sensible. In America, so many people cheer you on when you say that you are an entrepreneur with a dream. No other place is like that.

Unfortunately, I've seen a few successful entrepreneurs not being fully appreciative of the help they once received.

The behavior is understandable: Everyone tells them how great they are and how *they* did it all by themselves. Of course, at some point, they need to reflect and start appreciating the help they received and pay it forward.

I've heard Arnold Schwarzenegger, Mr. Universe turned movie star turned California governor, say, "Don't ever call me self-made, because I am not." He has often thanked people who advised him and helped him achieve his dreams.

I, myself, did not appreciate my mentors when I was younger. Now that I am older and slightly wiser, not a day goes by when I don't think about one of my many mentors. I could not be where I am today without their guidance and support. The best mentor I had was Bob Sayles who adopted me as his son when I was a homeless high school kid. He guided me and forgave me when I lost my way. Today, I am paying him back by mentoring others. I wish he were alive so that we could have a glass of his favorite whiskey together. On me, of course.

Takeaway: Be the kind of mentor that you wish you could have had.

47.

Plan on Giving It Away

"The meaning of life is to find your gift.
The purpose of life is to give it away."
– Pablo Picasso

One of the dumbest misconceptions I've encountered is the idea that wealthy individuals give because they have too much or feel guilty about their riches. Such misunderstandings trivialize the genuine generosity and sacrifices that donors make. Some assume it's easy to give if you are wealthy – these people don't have money. It takes tremendous character to give. It often takes time and effort to give effectively.

Over the years, as I've observed donors contributing to our school, I've developed a profound respect for them. I've come to realize that they are truly remarkable individuals. Many of the donors I encountered grew up without resources but worked hard to earn their wealth. Then, many of them lived pretty frugally for decades to save and eventually make selfless contributions. Their donations often go to strangers (people they don't know). Thus, most donors never receive a word of gratitude from the recipients.

I once enjoyed introducing a significant donor to his scholarship recipient. To my amazement, the person in tears with happiness was not the student, but the donor. In fact, I get disappointed with my students when they don't fully appreciate the scholarships they receive or feel they "deserve" them somehow.

In the U.S., we are fortunate to have thousands of generous individuals from whom to draw inspiration. One of my favorite entrepreneurs was Paul Newman, the iconic actor and race car driver who established Newman's Own, a salad dressing company. Remarkably, even after his passing, the company he founded continues to donate 100% of its profits, giving well over $500 million to various causes.

The science on giving is quite clear. There is joy in giving. There is also joy in winning after struggling. As an entrepreneur, you get to compete and win in the marketplace. After that, you can go about sharing your winnings and find an incredible amount of joy.

Congratulations on being blessed with entrepreneurial talent. Be that special person who shares their talent, time, and treasure with others, even those you don't know. Be a person of character. Be a hero. Plan on it.

Takeaway: Challenge yourself to share your time, talent, and treasures with others.

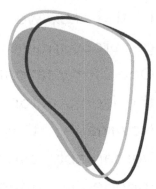

48.

Enjoy the Ride

"A successful life is a journey, not a destination."

– Arthur Ashe

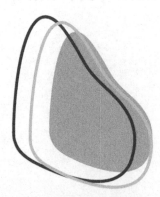

It's easy to assume that business success will bring happiness. However, numerous studies show that, if anything, the reverse is truer: When people are happy doing something, they are far more likely to find success because fun brings higher performance, better health, improved creativity, and enhanced focus.*

If I could go back in time, I would have tried to have more fun. Perhaps I had my share of fun in my earlier years, but over the last twenty-some years, I have been consumed by work and raising my children. It's easy to forget about having fun when all your focus is on accomplishments, no matter how noble the cause.

Even raising my children didn't feel enjoyable; it became a chore. My attention was fixated on the end goal of preparing them for adulthood, missing out on savoring those precious moments with them at the time. All of a sudden, my cute children are gone (grown-up), and I don't feel that I enjoyed those years as much as I should have.

We know that we should all relish the present, celebrate all victories, and take moments to enjoy life without going overboard. We must enjoy the journey, not just be obsessed with the destination.

It's a shame that I have seen so few of my good friends over the years, but I don't think I am the only person who has forgotten to do so.

Fortunately, these days, I have a couple of close friends who remind me to have fun. One is an impressive leader of his family business who consistently reminds his sons (also his business partners) to have fun and offers himself as an example. For him, fun is not just an expected outcome of their hard work, but also a to-do task to check off on a regular basis.

Takeaway: Cherish your journey. Make having fun a priority for you.

*Puca, R. M., & Schmalt, H. D. (1999). Task enjoyment: A mediator between achievement motives and performance. Motivation and Emotion, 23, 15-29.

The End

Congraulations!!!!

Made in the USA
Las Vegas, NV
18 November 2024